See Through Science

ACKNOWLEDGMENTS

Many people have been involved in the creation of this resource, and we are indebted to their generosity, hard work and honesty. Particular thanks go to following teachers who trialled the resource in their schools:

Madeleine Garczynski
Wimbledon High School

Penny Camburn
Coombe Hill Junior School

Sheetal Kowalczyk
Bromley High School

Katie Adams
Sheen Mount Primary School

Mandie Lambert
Holy Trinity C of E Primary School

Rachael Hourine
Alexandra School

Michelle McMahon
St Roch's Primary and Deaf School

Victoria Tyler
St Leonard's Primary School

Katie Scotland
Caledonia Primary School

Clare Keegan
Oakgrove Primary School

Kara Milliken
Shawlands Primary School

Colin Peebles
Mearns Primary School

The images in *See Through Science* have been taken from the following sources:

commons.wikimedia.org

pixabay.com

www.nasa.gov

www.photolib.noaa.gov

www.shutterstock.com

www.sciencephoto.com

Where necessary copyright has been purchased, so all images in the pack are licensed for teachers to use.

CONTENTS

FOREWORD

Images can take us to new environments: they can explore the very small, the very big, the instantaneous moment, and much more. Good scaffolding can allow young learners to immerse themselves in the images in ways that promote deep level exploration, raise good questions and of course, stimulate curiosity. The images collected and the supporting materials allow teachers to guide their children to *See Through Science*. Co-written by a PSTT Fellow in collaboration with a primary science advisory teacher, this book draws on many years of experience in teaching science at primary school level, providing an exciting gallery to explore.

Professor Dudley E. Shallcross
CEO, The Primary Science Teaching Trust

INTRODUCTION

As well as our ability to communicate complex ideas, an important trait that sets humans apart from other species is our innate curiosity. Since our evolution, we have tried to make sense of the world around us, its past and its possible futures. We observe things happening around us, often in complete awe, and ask questions. Why does the moon look different every night? How do flowers know when to grow? Where do stars come from? What happens to the water in a puddle?

We find ways to answer our questions, and then ask more questions with increasing complexity to build our knowledge of the world around us. We call this process 'science' and, without it, we wouldn't be where we are today. Medicine, sport, travel, communication, construction, finance, education, entertainment and many other fields all owe their current status to scientific advances.

In simple terms, without observation and questions there is no science, and without science there is no progression in our understanding of how everything around us works, and how it interacts with everything else.

Using a series of photographic images, *See Through Science* develops the skill of detailed observation that leads to scientific questioning and develops discussion and debate between children.

Each image is carefully selected to develop a range of observation skills, generate curiosity about the world around us, and prompt children to ask questions to further their understanding. The images reflect a range of scientific contexts to promote the importance of observation across different disciplines in science.

The images come with 'key questions' and also a set of supplementary questions to develop children's understanding further. Each image comes with a short explanation of the science depicted (with relevant weblinks), the background to the picture, and a list of key vocabulary.

This Teacher Guide explains the rationale for the concept of using photographic images to promote scientific questioning and discussion. It also provides ideas about how you might use the images in the classroom and in the wider school environment in a variety of different ways.

We hope you enjoy using *See Through Science*.

Alex Farrer and Paul Tyler

10 REASONS TO USE
SEE THROUGH SCIENCE

See Through Science:

Ignites children's curiosity

Increases understanding of context-specific scientific vocabulary and broadens scientific understanding

Promotes debate about scientific issues, encouraging children to collect evidence from observations to justify their opinions

Explores exciting worlds from the microscopic to inaccessible places on Earth and the far reaches of the Universe

Encourages precise observation of scientific detail

Provides opportunities for children to develop their thinking skills

Grows science capital by developing positive attitudes to science

Introduces lessons in an intriguing and engaging way, where answers are not immediately obvious

Assesses prior knowledge and addresses misconceptions that children have about many scientific phenomena

Develops teachers' confidence to facilitate discussions in science

WHAT DO TEACHERS SAY ABOUT
SEE THROUGH SCIENCE?

See Through Science has been trialled in 12 primary schools across the UK and the teachers' feedback has helped to shape the final resource. Here are some of their responses:

❝ These photos provide a fantastic hook to science lesson topics that are accessible to all the children. They inspire awe and wonder while developing questioning and explaining, as well as consolidating topic knowledge. As a bonus — it's fun! ❞

Mandie Lambert, Holy Trinity C of E Primary School

❝ The resource is so easy to pick up and run with! ❞

Kara Milliken, Shawlands Primary School

❝ These images helped spark scientific conversation in my class and around the school. It was an excellent way to assess children at the start and the end of a topic. The children were excited to find out about their new topic and there were excellent scientific words and vocabulary being used. ❞

Penny Camburn, Coombe Hill Junior School

❝ The photos in *See Through Science* have inspired and engaged children of all ages at our school. Children are highly engaged by the photos and very keen to share their knowledge and ideas. It gives them the opportunity to practise scientific language verbally before having to write about it. ❞

Katie Adams, Sheen Mount Primary School

❝ All classes involved showed improvement in their observational skills and the types of questions being created and used greatly improved. ❞

Michelle McMahon, St Roch's Primary and Deaf School

❝ The images gave me food for thought and inspired me to look at different stimuli for my learners. Learners engagement improved as well as my confidence in approaching the unknown and scientific world. ❞

Katie Scotland, Oakgrove Primary School

RATIONALE FOR
SEE THROUGH SCIENCE

WHY QUESTIONS?

In the introduction we established that questions are the starting point and foundations of science and if we are going to continue to develop our understanding, of pretty much everything, we need more people asking more questions (Chin & Osborne, 2008)[1].

Over thousands of years, as our ability to communicate has improved, so our questioning has improved. Our methods for finding answers and explaining those answers in terms that can be easily understood have also improved. If we want this trend of improvement to continue, we need to encourage our young people to ask questions and teach them how to turn their questions into scientific enquiries, so that they can find the answers and ask more questions.

Teachers' questions

Good questions asked by the teacher can:

- Elicit children's prior knowledge and personal experiences that relate to the science being taught;
- Support assessment of children's understanding of what they are being taught and whether they can explain it in simple terms;
- Identify children's misconceptions;
- Be used to stimulate discussion about the results of scientific investigation, helping children explain what happened and to identify reasons why something might have happened;
- Be used to spark debate about topical science issues encouraging children to generate ideas to conduct research, look critically at readings and articles, develop informed opinions and cite evidence to support their ideas;
- Be a safe way to discuss controversial scientific issues in class;
- Encourage children to listen to each other, consider other points of view and work together to improve their understanding about the topics that they are curious about; and
- Develop higher order thinking and encourage children to apply, analyse, justify and evaluate.

Children's scientific questions

Research suggests that, on average, teachers ask between 300 and 400 questions a day, whereas children ask one question a week (Graesser & Person, 1994; Levin & Long, 1981)[2]. What is it like in your classroom? How can you encourage your children to ask more questions?

The starting point for improving questioning in class is developing a safe environment and classroom ethos where children are happy to ask questions without fear. Some direct instruction and good modelling of asking good questions is needed, as well as many opportunities for the children to formulate their own questions in different contexts.

Modelling how to rephrase questions so that there is a measurable aspect to them will help children to generate investigable questions themselves. From these, they can then make hypotheses and predictions based on their observations and prior knowledge.

GOOD SCIENTIFIC QUESTIONS:

- Have real answers. The answer can be as simple as 'yes' or 'no', or it can be more detailed;
- Are testable. You can do an experiment or take measurements to find the answer;
- Are linked to a prediction or a hypothesis. This does not have to be correct; sometimes the investigation you carry out to test it will show that your it is false, and that is okay; and
- Are interesting!

❝ Effective learners ask questions; they tend to be people who remain curious and who approach life with 'wonderment and awe ❞
Murdoch (2011)[3]

[1]Chin, C. & Osborne, J. (2008) Students' questions: a potential resource for teaching and learning science. Studies in Science Education, 44 (1), 1-39

[2]Graesser, A. & Person, N. K. (1994). Questions asking during tutoring. American Educational Research Journal, (31), 104-137
Levin, T. & Long, R. (1981). Effective instruction. Washington, D.C.: Association for Supervision and Curriculum Development

[3]Murdoch, K. (2011) How do I get them to ask good questions? Retrieved from: www.learningnetwork.ac.nz/shared/professionalReading/KMWS62012.pdf

RATIONALE FOR
SEE THROUGH SCIENCE

WHY USE PHOTOGRAPHIC IMAGES?

Using carefully chosen photographic images is highly engaging for children and has many advantages over using other forms of media. Photographic images can take you to places where you couldn't normally go: inside a volcano, to the surface of Mars, into the Mariana Trench or to the Amazon rainforest.

They allow children to see unusual things in different contexts and because they are static, they enable children to focus on small and often unnoticed features. This leads to excellent opportunities for detailed observation, description and discussion. Using photographic images also gives the option to zoom in to see detail and zoom out to see the whole context. This allows children to study minute detail within a larger context. For encouraging observation of really fine detail, electron micrographs showing highly magnified objects or materials can be used. Micrographs open up a whole new and amazing world that children may never before have envisaged.

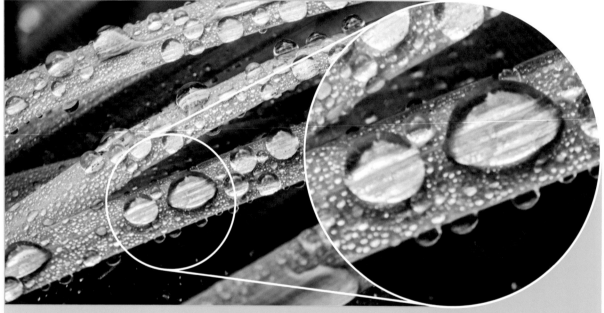

Images give the option to zoom in and explore in greater detail. This example shows how surface tension causes these water droplets to hold together, and that their resulting shape produces a magnifying effect that can be observed on the blade of grass.

Developing observation skills

Observation is a core scientific skill and needs to be taught and practised just like any other skill. It can be a challenge to develop as children are often afraid of being wrong or saying something too obvious. A photographic image can be a helpful way to build observation skills. Children can start by focusing on describing what they see, including colours, shapes and textures. Once they are confident with this, they can be encouraged to notice patterns and more complex detail, and relationships between different things

Using scientific vocabulary

Science, like many other subjects, has a language of its own. In fact, each separate scientific discipline has developed its own language, often with Latin and Greek roots, and many with a fascinating entomology. These word derivations are worth discussing with children as they can support a deeper understanding of the vocabulary, and can often help children remember it. For example, introducing the term 'photosynthesis' makes much more sense if you know that photo means to do with light and synthesis means put together. So, photosynthesis literally means 'put together with light'.

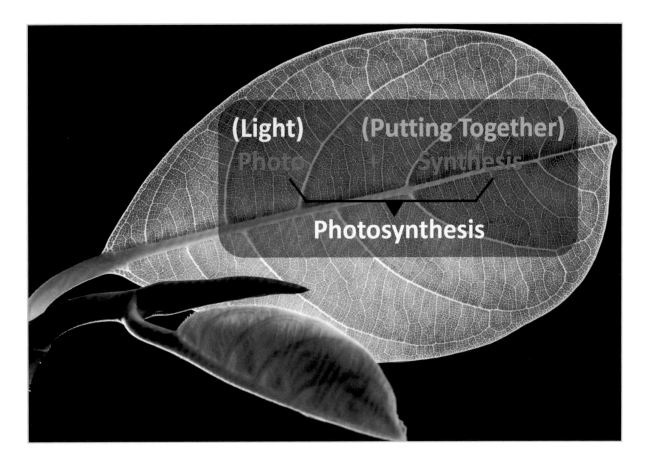

Children should be introduced to scientific vocabulary as early as possible. Many young children love learning new and complicated words and understanding what they mean. Once they are introduced to the vocabulary, they need to be given plenty of opportunity to practise using it to help reinforce its meaning and to apply it in new contexts.

RATIONALE FOR
SEE THROUGH SCIENCE

Addressing misconceptions

Children come to primary school with myriad science misconceptions and they are usually not shy in sharing them. It's important to develop an open class culture where children are happy to share their ideas – whether correct or incorrect – without feeling judged by their peers, teachers or other adults in the school.

Photographic images can provide powerful evidence to challenge children's existing ideas. It is more difficult for a child to disagree with others when they are all shown the same evidence.

A photo taken from the edge of space shows the curvature of the Earth's surface and can be used to help challenge misconceptions about the shape of our planet.

Making connections

As children's observation skills improve and they develop confidence in discussing their ideas and justifying them with evidence, they will be able to make more complex connections between their ideas.

Many of the photographic images in *See Through Science* can also be used to make links between science and other areas of the curriculum. Commonly there are links between science and physical education, health, technology and maths which can help children make connections to their lives and increase their understanding of the relevance of science.

A topic on World War 1 (WW1) can include looking at the technology, engineering and science of the day and analysing how good these are compared to the technology we have now. Comparisons can be made between images and similarities and differences observed and discussed.

By analysing the detail in photographic images, children build up an awareness of the complexity of both life on Earth and of human invention and engineering.

Many of the photographic images in *See Through Science* can also be used to make links between science and other areas of the curriculum. Commonly there are links between science and physical education, health, technology and maths which can help children make connections to their lives and increase their understanding of the relevance of science.

RATIONALE FOR
SEE THROUGH SCIENCE

How much science can you see in this image?
Children can be encouraged to make links to other areas of their lives through using images that are relevant to them.

Developing a critical eye

It is an interesting exercise to expose children to 'doctored' photos and ask them to decide if they are genuine or not. Evaluating evidence and building an opinion based on the evidence is important for understanding the limitations of images in any context.

Building science capital

Research has shown that children's science capital (by this we mean their existing science knowledge, their wider science experiences, their attitudes to science and the connections they have with others about science) is higher when there is high science capital at home (Archer, Osborne, DeWitt, Dillon, Wong, & Willis, 2013) . Using the photographic images in homework tasks to promote science discussion at home can help to build the science capital of the whole family.

Classroom Environment

The starting point for increasing science capital is to ensure that the children have a positive experience of science. Teachers need to create a classroom environment in which there is a range of scientific opportunities available to the children, and where their prior knowledge and ways of thinking and reasoning are valued. (Godec, King & Archer, 2017)[5].

Using photographic images in class offers very open opportunities for children to engage with science, and to share prior knowledge about a topic. Working in small groups ensures that all children get an opportunity to express their ideas and opinions.

Career links

The *See Through Science* photographic images provide opportunities to discuss STEM careers in a variety of ways. Discussing who might have taken the photo and why they took it gives an insight into the range of careers that exist, as well as highlighting the importance of photography as a way of recording, classifying and examining scientific findings. Photographic images of scientists in situ can be an inspiring way of introducing children to careers that they may not have heard of before.

A volcanologist in full protective gear samples a lava flow using a hammer and bucket to collect lava for chemical analysis.

Relevance

If science is relevant to children's lives and their everyday experiences, it is more likely to capture their interest and have a lasting impact. This supports the development of their science capital and the likelihood of them engaging with science in the longer term.

See Through Science deliberately includes photographic images of everyday objects or experiences shown in unusual ways. This is to provide opportunities for linking the science being taught to the children's own experiences and to help them understand the importance and relevance of science to their lives.

Inspiration

The photographic images have been carefully selected to inspire, or to intrigue, or to make children go 'WOW!' and want to find out more.

Links to the wider community

Using the images beyond the classroom (e.g. round the school, on a school website or as homework) can increase family engagement in science. Photos can be linked to topical science that is in the news, and relevant questions can be posed to promote discussion and debate.

[4]Archer, L., Osborne, J., DeWitt, J., Dillon, J., Wong, B. & Willis, B. (2013). ASPIRES: Young people's science and career aspirations, age 10–14. London: King's College London

[5]Godec, S. King, H. & Archer, L. (2017). The Science Capital Teaching Approach: engaging students with science, promoting social justice. London: University College London

QUICK START GUIDE

See Through Science is designed to be a flexible resource that can be used in class, with small groups, in assemblies, at home or around the school. This four-page section gives an overview of how to start using the resource. For more detailed ideas and applications please see Additional ideas for making the most of *See Through Science* on page 21.

THE PHOTOGRAPHIC IMAGE PACK

The image pack comes as a pdf that you need to download from: **pstt.org.uk/STS-imagepack**

The pack includes 15 photographic images. The first page of the pack shows thumbnail pictures of each of the images; clicking on one of these will take you straight to the title slide for the section about that image. The resources for each image consist of the following pages:

Image on its own

Image with the key question

The key question is designed to be used in class to promote discussion and support children with developing their own questioning skills.

Image with a key question to use when displayed around the school or in newsletters

Image as a printable placemat

This can be used to encourage groups of children to collaborate and collect their ideas and questions by writing or drawing them around the edge of the image.

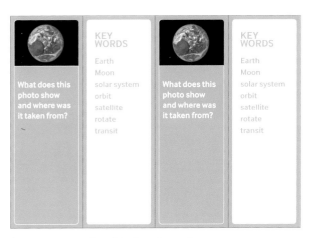

Image as a printable bookmark

The bookmark shows the image with the key question on one side, and a list of the key vocabulary on the other. This can be printed, folded and laminated for children to use to during lessons and in any follow-up work.

Image with supporting information for the teacher

This includes the key background information, links to suggestions for finding out further information, the key vocabulary and a set of supplementary questions. It also offers an idea for a practical activity to extend children's learning.

QUICK START GUIDE

ASKING QUESTIONS

To promote discussion that will enable children to make progress with their scientific understanding requires the teacher to ask good questions. The teacher can also support the children with asking increasingly complex scientific questions of their own.

Different types of question that the teacher could ask

What is this?	Children discuss in pairs what they think the image shows. They decide on three very convincing reasons as to why they are sure of their answer. Again, the focus should be on the reasons given for the answer rather than the answer itself.
What is happening / has happened / might happen next here?	Children discuss in pairs events that they think might have happened in relation to the image. Ask them to decide on three very convincing reasons to justify their suggestions.
What are the key words?	Children come up with key words that could be used to search for the image online. Children can also be asked to decide on five key scientific words that the image makes them think of. At the end of the lesson they return to their key word list to see if the words were the ones they used in the lesson and if any need to be added or removed.
Odd one out	Which is the odd one out and why? Focus on the why rather than any one right answer, and make sure the children justify their choice with clear reasoning.
Similarities and differences	What is similar about the images and what is different – why do you think that might be?

What is the title?	Children think, pair, share to come up with possible titles for the image – they need to be able to justify their ideas.
What are the learning objectives?	Children can be asked to decide on the key learning objectives that they think will be relevant for the lesson based on the image. At the end of the lesson they return to their learning objectives to see if they were the objectives addressed in the lesson or not.
How does this make you feel?	Children discuss the image in terms of how it makes them feel and why it makes them feel like that.
What do you already know about this?	Children are asked to make a list of all that they already know about what they see in the image.
What have you found out about this image?	Children are asked to make a list of all that they have learned about what they see in the image.
Research and opinion questions	The images can be used round the school, or at home, with more specific questions attached to them. These are either for children to find something out or contribute an opinion or thought.
Topical science questions	Many of the images can be linked to science in the news and questions can relate to what the specific link is and what its relevance is.

QUICK START GUIDE

Supporting the children with asking their own scientific questions

Yes/No questions	Children in pairs or small groups have five minutes to decide on a set of questions they want to ask – they must be able to be answered with a YES or a NO. The teacher answers 'YES' or 'NO' to questions from six different groups, with the whole class hearing the questions and answers. Using this information, each group must decide what they think the image is. If they cannot work it out, the teacher can answer further questions.
What is the question?	Children have an image in front of them that they are told is the answer to a question. They are then asked to suggest a possible question. This is a challenging task and it is useful to try out a few examples first.
What would you like to know about this?	Children discuss in pairs what they would like to know about this image. Ask them to record their questions and think about how they would find out the answers.

MORE SUGGESTIONS FOR HELPING CHILDREN ASK BETTER QUESTIONS

Make sure the children sometimes see you as a learner too by modelling good learning habits yourself: asking questions, researching, experimenting, evaluating, analysing, verifying and critiquing information.

Model a balance of open and closed questions to draw out knowledge and develop understanding. Open questions allow an opportunity to expand on basic knowledge, give examples and explain what is understood. Closed questions can be used to demonstrate knowledge and can be a useful bridge between a series of open questions.

Value every question that the children ask, even if it might not have been what you expected. If children feel their questions are being ignored or constantly rephrased, they will be reluctant to ask them.

Ask some questions that require an opinion rather than just facts, or right or wrong answers. This can create a more tolerant and collaborative classroom culture and encourage a more diverse range of responses.

Don't be afraid to include some direct teaching about how to ask 'scientific' questions, especially with younger children. They will have the curiosity but not always the vocabulary or understanding to frame the question in a scientific way. Model asking scientific questions when children are carrying out investigations, help them rephrase their questions and add in technical vocabulary when necessary.

Phrase questions to make them less threatening and allow the children to feel that they are making a more personal response rather than having to produce a correct idea, e.g. instead of asking, 'Why does that happen?' try asking, 'Why do you think that happens?' This difference is subtle, but it is important.

Use opportunities to build on the children's questions. Ask supplementary questions to probe for deeper understanding, encourage further research to develop knowledge of concepts and if appropriate, leave questions tantalisingly unanswered to keep children curious.

Use paired or group discussion to take the pressure off individuals and encourage collaborative thinking. The placemat resource will encourage groups to share their ideas and construct questions together.

Use post-it notes for the occasions when children might think of a question when they are engaged in an activity or cannot share it with others very easily. It is difficult to predict when questions are going to pop into your head and this is especially true for children whose focus can switch rapidly between different stimuli, leading them to make unusual connections between things. Questions on post-it-notes can make a very effective 'question wall'. Children write their question down and stick the post-it note up on the wall to be revisited at a later time.

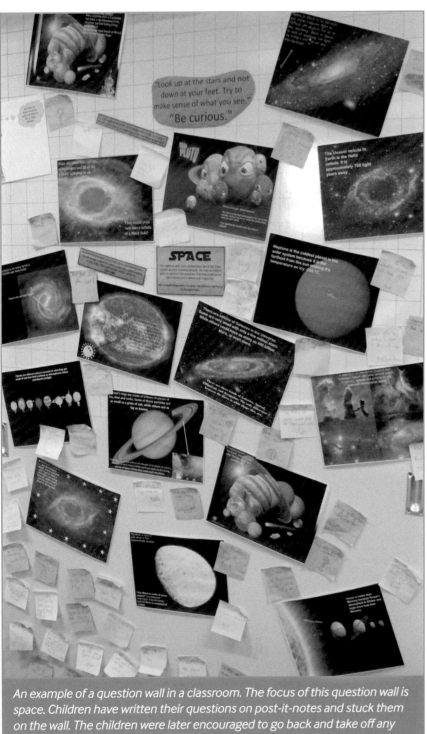

An example of a question wall in a classroom. The focus of this question wall is space. Children have written their questions on post-it-notes and stuck them on the wall. The children were later encouraged to go back and take off any questions that they wanted to research.

ADDITIONAL IDEAS FOR MAKING THE MOST OF *SEE THROUGH SCIENCE*

The images in *See Through Science* are supplied in a digital format to allow versatility in how you use them in school. This section includes a range of suggestions about how to make the most of using the photographic images.

IMPROVING OBSERVATION SKILLS

Micrographs and photographs that show close-ups enable children to look more closely at objects and notice finer details. Show the close-up first and ask children what they think it is and why they think this. Then gradually zoom out to reveal more of the whole picture to show the close-up detail in its full context.

This kind of detailed observation can maintain children's curiosity and encourage them to want to carry out additional research to build on their ideas. For example, a micrograph of a fly's compound eye might lead to children wanting to know what benefit this kind of eye gives the fly, what other animals have eyes like this, and what the world would look like through one. Further research will give answers to many of their questions.

Compound eyes of a Robber Fly. Micrographic images like this open up a whole unseen world which can lead to excellent discussions and interesting questions being asked.

Scientific observation is about finding clues, either to ask or to answer questions. Encourage children to notice all the detail in an image, however trivial it might seem. Finding the answer often relies on piecing together small clues to form the whole picture. Almost as important as being able to make accurate observations is being able to share them and discuss them. Science communication is an essential part of children's development as curious, collaborative scientists.

ADDITIONAL IDEAS FOR MAKING THE MOST OF *SEE THROUGH SCIENCE*

Try this!

This is a great activity to develop observation skills and encourage the children to focus on noticing detail. Give every child a chocolate chip cookie and ask them to draw it. Once they have all done this, mix the cookies up and ask the children to use their detailed drawing to identify their own cookie.

Close observation of the chocolate chip cookie leads to a detailed diagram which can then be used to identify the cookie when it is mixed up with many similar looking cookies. Children need to be explicitly taught how to observe closely and notice details that might be important.

ADDITIONAL IDEAS FOR MAKING THE MOST OF *SEE THROUGH SCIENCE*

Observation activities and targeted questioning are excellent for identifying misconceptions.

Some suggestions:

- Set an observation task and listen in to paired or group discussions where children are more likely to speak openly.

- Listen to the children's ideas, and listen specifically for any misconceptions they appear to have.

- Make a note of any misconceptions that you might be able to address with the class. Often if one child has a misconception then others will too, but they may not all be willing to express what they are thinking.

- Ask the children to write or draw their ideas or observations and collect what they have recorded so that you can assess their current thinking.

- Try not to dismiss children's ideas, even if you know they are wrong. Often misconceptions are quite deeply held and may have come from someone the child respects. Dismissing an idea can cause resentment and disengagement.

- Remember that it can take a long time for a child to change a deeply held idea, even if others are disagreeing or they can see evidence that does not support what they think.

- Provide evidence of correct ideas and let the children work out the truth for themselves through observation, questioning and their own research.

GENERATING LESSON IDEAS

The images can be used as a starting point for science as part of a topic. They can be used to find out what children already know and to generate questions about things they would like to find out. Several of the images have simple key questions, e.g. 'What questions would you ask about this?' and are designed to get children using their observations to formulate their own scientific questions.

The questions that the children generate from looking at the images can act as a stimulus for planning practical investigations and additional research into a topic.

The images can also be used to focus on specific areas of lessons. For example, the picture of the Venus fly trap could be a stimulus for work on the structure of flowering plants, using specific questions to check understanding and identify misconceptions.

PROMOTING DISCUSSION AND DEBATE

The images can be used to develop children's ability to ask scientific questions, and to talk and debate about science in different contexts. Children can work collaboratively to explore an image and talk about what they know about it, what they can deduce from it, what they want to know about it, and the vocabulary that they associate with it.

The printable placemats are an ideal way to encourage children to collaborate, sharing ideas vocabulary and questions.

ADDITIONAL IDEAS FOR MAKING THE MOST OF *SEE THROUGH SCIENCE*

When groups are giving feedback about their discussions, encourage other children to listen carefully, take notes, and ensure that they have an opportunity to respond. Scientists constantly offer respectful challenges to each other's ideas. You can model this process with children and encourage them to start challenging each other to justify their thinking.

See Through Science can be used not just for developing better scientific understanding, but also for developing better group work skills. If groups are struggling to work collaboratively, they are less likely to make scientific progress, but if the children are encouraged to use the activity to focus on working constructively as a group this will pay dividends for future activities.

USING EVIDENCE TO JUSTIFY IDEAS

Being able to explain clearly and justify ideas and opinions are key skills in science. The photographic images can be a very effective source of evidence for children to formulate ideas and suggestions, and as a basis for research in order to gather further evidence, refine their own thinking and then present their evidence-based ideas to the class. Groups could be given different photographic images to work on before sharing and discussing with their peers.

MOVING FROM QUESTION TO PREDICTION AND HYPOTHESIS

Good scientific questions often lead to a prediction or a hypothesis that is testable through experimentation and measurement. The children might need repeated modelling of developing a question into something that can be investigated.

The first three questions are all good scientific questions. They are all testable by experimentation and can be measured. They can lead to the formation of a prediction about what the answer might be which in turn can lead to the development of a hypothesis.

The fourth question is still a good question but, in its current form, it cannot be answered by experimentation or measuring. If it is rephrased as 'Is rubber the best material to make tyres from?' it then becomes a question that can lead to a prediction that can be tested, which could lead to a hypothesis about why rubber is the best material.

It's important to point out to children that not all the questions they generate will be able to be tested in school. Many of them will require specialist equipment (like a Formula 1 car!) or might be dangerous to carry out. However, the chances are that someone somewhere will have carried out the experiment at some point, so even if they cannot do it themselves, the children might be able to find an example of it by looking on the internet.

A photographic image like this might prompt questions like:

1. *How fast can a Formula 1 car drive?*
2. *How much faster can it drive in the dry than in the wet?*
3. *Do the brakes work better in dry or wet conditions?*
4. *Why are tyres made of rubber?*

ENCOURAGING CRITICAL LITERACY

The photographic images can be used to develop children's critical literacy skills, by asking them to question the validity and credibility of images. This is especially important now that technology exists for the easy manipulation of images, which changes their integrity. Encourage children to question what they are seeing and conduct further research to validate the evidence they have.

You could introduce children to the importance of knowing whether or not to trust a photographic image through a 'True or False?' activity. Give the children an image with some explanatory text. If the image is a true image, the accompanying text you give could be true or false, and if the image is a false image, the text you give will therefore also be false. Ask the children to decide if the image and text are true or false and why they think this.

This 'wild haggis' example is of a false image with false text:

The wild haggis is only found in remote areas of Scotland. It has one leg longer than the other so it can easily run around the steep slopes of the Highlands.

Can children use their observation, questioning and research skills to discover the truth about this beautiful, rare animal?

ADDITIONAL IDEAS FOR MAKING THE MOST OF *SEE THROUGH SCIENCE*

RAISING THE PROFILE OF SCIENCE

Posting the photographic images on school websites or in school newsletters with questions and follow-up activities and research tasks is an excellent way to engage children and their families and develop their science capital.

Talk Topics

The whole school will be involved in a weekly Talk Topic during the fortnight. We would appreciate if you would take time to discuss the talk topic and help your child to gather a variety of views from parents, grandparents and friends. On Thursday or Friday of each week, pupils will share their ideas and views during a class circle time.

Week 1 Talk Topic: Life Below Water

Look at the pictures above and read the fact …

'It's thought there will be more plastic than fish (by weight) in the sea by 2050.'

How does this make you feel? Is it hard to avoid single use plastic in our everyday lives?
What simple change could you make to help Planet Earth?
Would you and your family consider supporting the Earth Hour Event on Saturday, 24 March?
Follow the link below to see what other people have promised:
World Wildlife Fund - A Pledge for our Planet

Using images to engage families in discussion of environmental issues as part of a talking homework task.

Children discussing an image displayed in the playground. This can be followed up by teachers in class.

Specific home learning tasks linking images to the science being learnt at school can be used to consolidate understanding and as an inspiration for further research or practical investigation.

Posting images in communal areas of the school, for example facing out into the playground is a great way to encourage informal science discussion among children and parents. A different image can be used each week with teachers following up the discussion in class during the week.

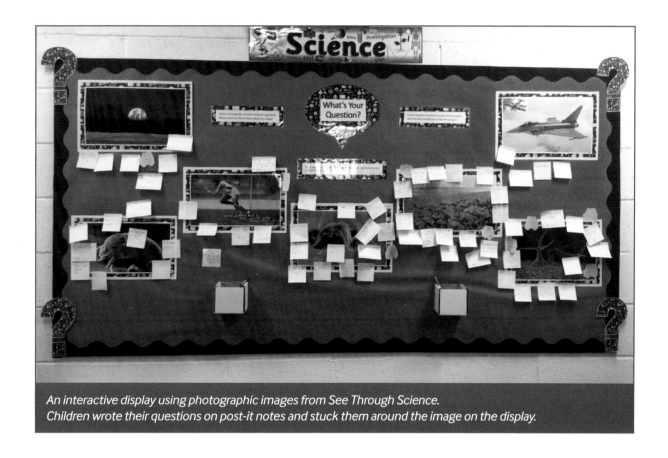

An interactive display using photographic images from See Through Science.
Children wrote their questions on post-it notes and stuck them around the image on the display.

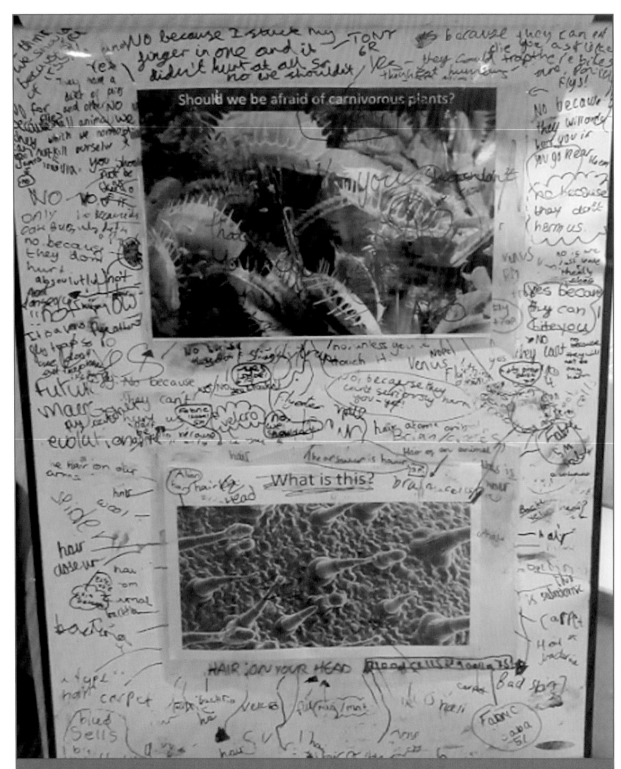

Photographic images from See Through Science displayed on a whiteboard in the lunch hall. Children wrote up their ideas and thoughts while they were waiting for lunch. This led to some interesting and spontaneous discussions between children.

GENERATING AWE AND WONDER

The images have been chosen to be inspirational and generate awe and wonder about science. They can be used in assemblies or during science weeks to create a buzz about science throughout the school.

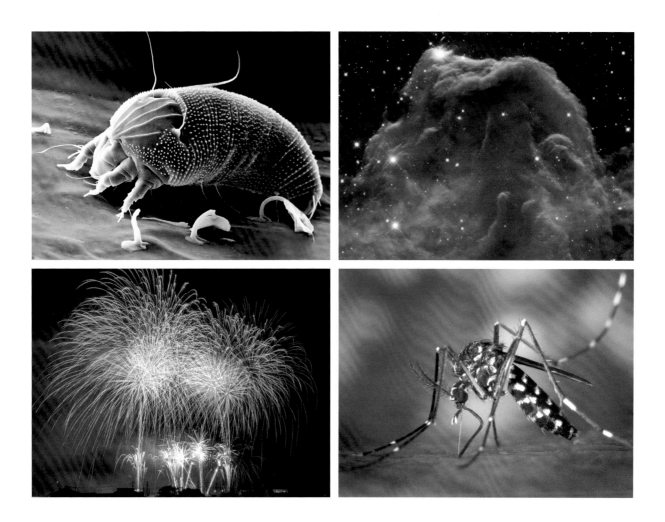

WHERE WILL *SEE THROUGH SCIENCE* TAKE YOU NEXT?

RECOMMENDED READING

Archer, L., Osborne, J., DeWitt, J., Dillon, J., Wong, B. & Willis, B. (2013).
ASPIRES: Young people's science and career aspirations, age 10–14. London: King's College London

Chin, C. (2001). Learning in Science: What Do Students' Questions Tell Us About Their Thinking?
Education Journal 《教育學報》 **29** (2), Winter 2001

Chin, C. (2004). Students' questions: fostering a culture of inquisitiveness in science classrooms.
School Science Review, **86** (314), 107–112

Chin, C. & Osborne, J. (2008) Students' questions: a potential resource for teaching and learning science.
Studies in Science Education, **44** (1), 1-39

Dedicott, W. (1987). *The Value of Pictures in Encouraging Children's Thinking Strategies.*
Reading: The United Kingdom Literacy Association, **21** (1)

Godec, S. King, H. & Archer, L. (2017). The Science Capital Teaching
Approach: engaging students with science, promoting social justice. London: University College London

Graesser, A. & Person, N. K. (1994). Questions asking during tutoring. *American Educational Research Journal*, (31), 104-137

Levin, T. & Long, R. (1981) *Effective instruction*. Washington, D. C.: Association for Supervision and Curriculum Development

Murdoch, K. (2011) *How do I get them to ask good questions?* Retrieved from:
www.learningnetwork.ac.nz/shared/professionalReading/KMWS62012.pdf

Rivett, A.C., Harrison, T.G. & Shallcross, D.E. (2009). The Art of Chemistry. Primary Science Review, **110**, 9-13.